Communication Is At The Core Of Every Business And Relationship

A Short Course

Online Trainees

Content

Communication

Communication is at the core of every business. Without effective communication no business can thrive and grow.

The challenge of effective communication is one we all face.

In 1948 Dr Albert Einstein declined the invitation to become the first president of the new state of Israel. The greatest conceptual and technical genius of his time declined on the grounds that he was not qualified for any position which required an understanding of human relationships, including clear communication.

Communication is the main means by which people can build relationships in the workplace and elsewhere. It is estimated that more than 90% of today's leaders fail to communicate with their employees in a manner necessary for building relationships based on mutual trust and respect.

Without effective communication employees get frustrated and often leave resulting in more money that has to be spend on training new staff.

Written and oral communication skills are critical in securing work and also in performing effectively in your work, and maintaining crucial business relationships.

Dialogue is the main means of getting our ideas across. Oral communication is something we do all day, every day. Consequently it is something we take completely for granted.

Many misunderstandings occur from poor choice of words, tone or body language. In the communication process it is the duty of the speaker to ensure that the listener has a clear understanding of what we are trying to communicate.

Clarify Communication

Developing your questioning skills will assist you to clarify and develop a clear understanding of the subject under discussion.

Questions are important for use during any conversation where a person has expressed his/her feelings or point of view.

Too many questions in a session may seem like an interrogation and lead to defensiveness.

Leading questions that put answers into people's mouths should be avoided. The listener may be left with the impression that you already have decided what the answer should be.

Closed questions allow the speaker to respond with only one word answers. Although these questions can be used to obtain valuable information, clarity or focus, overuse of them should be avoided. In a sales environment it can be detrimental to use closed questions – you need to create a positive two way communication.

Open questions create opportunities for expanding on responses and focus on the process rather than the person. It makes the listener feel more relaxed and responsive.

Questions that probe too deeply tend to arouse anxiety and resistance. People often get uncomfortable and view it as an invasion of privacy.

Badly timed questions can lead to emotional outbursts during a discussion and it is counter productive to question them at great length.

"Why" questions can be perceived as insulting, since they imply doubt or criticism of a person's motives.

Rhetorical questions are not really a question, as they do not require an answer.

Enlarging questions have the purpose of identifying certain details, which will help a person understand a problem more clearly. The listener will feel you are interested in their input.

It is important to use questions effectively or it may be difficult to understand complex issues under discussion.

Encouragement Or Repetition

Encouragement or repetition is used primarily to encourage the person to elaborate a little further.

Short remarks such as "hmmm", "tell me more" and "is that so" are examples. It implies to the speaker that you understand and want them to continue.

Listening

Research has shown that people spend about 45% of their communication time listening. Despite this, the average listener understands and retains about half of what is said immediately, and within 48 hours this level drops down to 22%. Most people will listen to what is being said, but do not actually hear and understand the message that is being conveyed.

Listening is therefore one of the most critical skills in the communication process. It helps to determine the others needs, problems, moods or levels of interest.

In order to become effective communicators, we need to tune in, not only to words and the way words are expressed, but to non verbal cues as well.

Active Listening

Active or reflective listening is a method of responding to people and enables us to concentrate on their meaning, without using judgemental or analytical comments and questions. It gives us the best chance of discovering their intentions when they communicate with us, rather than merely making assumptions about what they mean.

Use Your Ears

Explore by asking questions.

Affirm to show you are listening.

Reflect your understanding.

Silence. Listen some more.

Active listening consists of rephrasing the crucial parts of what someone says to you and repeating it to the speaker. It is important to use your own words, based on your understanding of what the person has said, rather than just repeating what they have said. They are fed back as statements, not questions, keeping you within the person's permitted space. A good tool is to make note of key phrases whilst the other person is speaking taking care not to get so caught up in making notes that you lose track of what is being said.

Speaker: "...and I don't really get on with them"

You: "... You feel you have little in common"

This form of listening would seem very odd if you did it for everything someone said, therefore only use it occasionally.

When To Use

If you are not sure what the person really means.

If someone has said something with real feeling and emotion in their voice.

If someone is talking about their feelings and/or emotions.

If someone is talking about a personal matter or problem.

These four occasions arise continuously in our work and social life. Unfortunately, the interference of criticism, sympathy and analytic responses are used most often in these situations and are least likely to create empathy.

The advantages of using active listening as an assertive communication skill are:

It prevents misunderstanding – it allows the speaker to check the listener's interpretation of their meaning.

It shows acceptance of the speaker – it is not critical, sympathetic or analytical but empathetic. If your reflected statement is accurate it shows that you are on the same wavelength as the speaker, and have understood what they are saying without being judgemental.

It defuses emotion – by being sympathetic, it helps people feel understood. This has a calming effect on their feelings in a manner that critical, sympathetic and analytical behaviour cannot do.

It leaves the problem with the speaker as you are not making any attempt to take over and answer another person's problems unless invited to.

With the active listening technique you understand the speaker's problems and how they feel about them. When this is done it is amazing how often this releases the speaker's ability to solve his/her own problems. Very often, by just verbalising our problems we will be able to find our own solutions.

Guidelines For Active Listening

The listener should reflect the speaker's feelings in his/her own words rather than serve as a mimic or repeat everything in parrot fashion.

Remarks should start with:

I feel

I think

It seems to me that

Reflected statements should be phrased as statements not as questions.

It is important not to be afraid of pauses. The speaker may be trying to sort out his/her own thoughts and may be on the verge of expressing them when the listener breaks in with a question or comment.

When feelings are being expressed, only the last one should be reflected. It is dangerous for the listener to start guessing at feelings he/she thinks should be there.

When inconsistent feelings are expressed the listener should act as if no inconsistency has taken place.

Elements Of Effective Communication

Words:

Words combine to form the phrases or statements that we use to express the thoughts that we intend to communicate.

They include:

Vocabulary

Language

Phrases

Sentence structure

Sentence clarity

Words can soothe, insult or injure and can lead to costly errors, false hopes, or disillusionment. They evoke pride, loyalty, action or silence. However, they are not the sole basis for how people represent and interpret reality.

Paralanguage:

Paralanguage is the characteristics of the voice such as:

Rate of speech

Diction

Tone

Rhythm

Volume

Your voice is a highly versatile instrument. Through it you can convey enthusiasm, confidence, anxiety, urgency etc. The ability of how the voice affect something that is said is known as paralanguage. By paying close attention to the other person's paralanguage, you can pick up clues about what they are really thinking.

Nonverbal Behaviour

Nonverbal behaviour is anything that can be "seen" by the other person such as:

Gestures

Facial expressions

Eye contact

Body language

Positioning

How you enter an office, how you support your message through gestures and facial expressions, how you imply interest and vitality through eye contact and other non verbal cues can affect other people's reaction to you. In turn their non-verbal behaviour serves as a window to their emotions, thoughts and attitudes.

When communicating with other people, the spoken message passes through perceptual filters creating the potential for a communication breakdown at any point in the process.

It is as if "I know you think you understand what I said, but I am not sure that what you heard is what I meant".

Key Points

Make yourself clear.

Plan before you speak

Do not interrupt

Keep it simple

Be specific

Get feedback

Power Of Behaviour

Have you thought about how you communicate and what your communication style says about you?

Most people are content with their ability to deal successfully with a majority of people and situations. It is the difficult ones that matter. You need to be able to communicate in an assertive manner, and adapt your communication style to theirs.

We can all recall occasions where we wished we had handled a situation differently, where we felt that we should have spoken up when we remained silent, or where we lost our temper and said more than we should have. Whatever the circumstances, these situations leave us feeling uncomfortable. We feel helpless and frustrated. Why did we remain silent? What was it that stopped us from speaking our mind? What made us lose our temper?

Let us assume that you have already made plans for the evening, but at the last minute your manager asks you to work on a rush job. Would you:

Say nothing to your manager about your plans and simply agree to work late to finish the job.

Refuse your manager in no uncertain terms, complaining about his lack of planning.

Explain that you will not be able to work late this evening because you have made special plans, but could you arrive early the next morning to complete the work.

The three responses characterise very different communication styles and behaviours. The first response illustrates a passive communication style, the second an aggressive communication style, and the last an assertive communication style.

Whether you are responding to someone else's behaviour or initiating some action yourself, you will have four principle options on how you choose to behave. You can use:

Submissive/Passive Behaviour

You allow others to control your behaviour.

Accept all criticism as valid and feel guilty, and even apologetic, when you have to criticise others.

You conceal your feelings and desires, and always try to please others.

Aggressive Behaviour

You make your feelings known – often to the point of disregarding other people's feelings.

You are dominating and insensitive, leaving others feeling resentful, angry and put down.

Assertive Behaviour

You express yourself in an open, honest, straightforward, and direct manner.

You stand up for your rights without violating the rights of others.

Passive Aggressive

You express your aggression in a passive manner.

You believe that nobody has any right to freely express their feelings.

You often respond in a sarcastic or manipulative manner.

Assertiveness is often confused with aggressiveness. There is a big difference between these two concepts however. It is useful to think of a continuum along which the whole range of human behaviour lies. Some behaviour is extremely passive, some is extremely aggressive, and assertive lies somewhere in between.

Improving Interpersonal Communication Effectiveness

Assertiveness and the ability to influence people is not going to solve all your problems, or make your relationships successful. These skills are concerned with being happier with yourself, and in your relationships in life. They are also concerned with treating people as they want to be treated and at the same time, respecting yourself as you do others. It does not involve a constant attempt to be assertive in all that you say and do; rather it involves a choice of behaviour options to suit situations.

People today are more concerned with outward appearances. There are multimillion businesses in cosmetics and diet. Many people spend hours on their outward appearance and getting themselves in shape. Often using methods that seem like torture, solely so that they can portray the exact image that they want to project. However, the lasting impressions that people make are based on their behaviour – what they say and what they do.

We belong to different social classes, age groups, ethnic groups etc that to some extent dictate our dress, our speech patterns, our standards and norms, but when we judge each other as people within these classifications, it is according to our social and communication skills. We give people respect and therefore authority, according to how they handle people and situations.

You must establish a personal need to learn any skills that may be new to you. Many of us develop our skills in the same way as we learn to play a musical instrument: by stages. There are always people with exceptional talent who can acquire skills without much effort, but for most of us we have to practice very hard.

For many of us, there is a parallel experience as adults learning to drive a car. The many individual actions that we have to take before starting a car and moving off are terribly difficult for most of us to learn at first. Frequently an essential is overlooked. Once we have passed our test, and gained valuable driving experience, we find that we can drive while talking to another person or listening to music on the radio. We have absorbed the detailed actions, which we consciously repeated so many times, and, by just willing the result of the action, our unconscious mind will follow the required program.

The same principles apply to learning life skills. Some of these may be inherent, as with some non-verbal communication, or easily acquired. For the majority of us, learning most life skills, including assertion, requires the same conscious effort as learning to drive before we can use them unconsciously.

Using Assertiveness

Choose a safe relationship and situation

Practice

Develop the skills in easy stages

We are not born with effective communication skills: we need to develop them. This course was designed to help you gain as much knowledge about assertive communication as possible. This will make you more aware of your own interpersonal skills that may need improvement. Most importantly, it is necessary for you to practice these skills as frequently as possible.

Keep in mind the following aspects of learning a new skill:

When you learn a new skill, you will feel strange, self-conscious and awkward.

Practising your skill may feel phoney or insincere.

The process may seem somewhat mechanical and unreal.

In time, the skill will become fully integrated in your behavioural repertoire and it will seem a natural action to engage in.

Assertive Managers

The best managers are open and direct communicators, able to express their feelings, needs, and wants to others. Managers tend to get results when they unambiguously communicate their goals and objectives. Energy is often wasted defending and attacking, when in reality, goal-orientated behaviour usually works best.

People with assertive communication styles are comfortable with themselves and others are likely to be comfortable with them and will not feel threatened by them. They will not be derogatory about the other person, use verbal attacks, or exploitation. Rather they communicate in a straightforward manner. Assertive managers are respected by their staff. Openness begets trust and builds confidence.

Assertiveness is the ability to express yourself and your rights without violating the rights of others.

It encourages direct, open and honest communication which is self-enhancing and expressive.

Acting assertively will allow you to feel self-confident and will generally gain you the respect of your peers and friends. It can increase your chances for honest relationships, and help you feel better about yourself and to maintain your self-control in everyday situations. This, in turn will improve your decision making ability and your chances of getting what you really want from life.

Patterns Of Behaviour Questionnaire

We all use different types of behaviour to suit different situations. The aim with the questions below is to help you understand which behaviour you normally use in certain situations so that you can get an indication of the behaviour you prefer. This exercise should give you an idea of your instinctive behaviour that could affect your relationships.

1). Do you have difficulty expressing your real feelings to others?

Yes / No

2). Do you often feel that others manipulate you?

Yes / No

3). Do you usually keep quiet when someone jumps the queue in front of you?

Yes / No

4). Do you keep quiet or only complain to your friends and colleagues?

Yes / No

5). Do you often find yourself doing tasks you do not really want to do?

Yes / No

6). Do you find it difficult to stand up to seniors, supervisors and authorities when you disagree with them

Yes / No

7). Do you avoid confronting people because you have to work with them. Tomorrow, or because you do not want to upset or anger them

Yes / No

8). Do you prefer to give subtle hints to people about your wishes?

Yes / No

9). Are there any situations in life where you really would like to speak your mind?

Yes / No

10).Do you often seem to change your mind to go along with the majority of a powerful group when you really do not agree with them?

Yes / No

11). Do you believe "anything for a quiet life"?

Yes / No

12). Do you find it difficult to cope with aggressive verbal behaviour?

Yes / No

130. If attacked verbally do you resort to making excuses?

Yes / No

14). Are there many situations which you suffer in silence, to which you have resigned yourself?

Yes / No

Questionnaire B

1). Do you like to speak your mind openly, even if it may give offence to others?

Yes / No

2). Would you describe yourself as blunt and to the point?

Yes / No

3). Do you often get into arguments with others that are not resolved?

Yes / No

4). Do you easily lose your temper?

Yes / No

5). Are you always ready to complain?

Yes / No

6). Do you get angry and tell him/her off when someone jumps the queue in front of you?

Yes / No

7). Do you tell people who annoy you to shut up?

Yes / No

8). Do you find yourself putting people down?

Yes / No

9). Do you tend to keep others waiting for you without any apology or reason?

Yes / No

10). Do you criticise and find fault with others openly?

Yes / No

11). Do you regularly try and get one up on people?

Yes / No

12). Do you feel that if you are reasonable with people you will probably end up giving something away?

Yes / No

13). If attacked verbally do you resort to attacking the other person?

Yes / No

14). Do you normally try very hard to get your solutions to other people's problems accepted

Yes / No

Questionnaire C

1). Can you express your feelings openly and honestly to people?

Yes / No

2). Do you mix equally easily with superiors, peers and subordinates – do you acknowledge their point of view?

Yes / No

3). Do you try and see the other person's point of view in arguments and discussions?

Yes / No

4). Do you keep your temper in check when other people attack you?

Yes / No

5). Do you find you can resolve most problems that other people cause without damaging your relationship?

Yes / No

6). Is the relationship better afterwards?

Yes / No

7). Do you normally deal with your concerns and those of others rather than ignoring them or diverting them?

Yes / No

8). Do you try and resolve differences with people by bringing them out Into the open?

Yes / No

9). Do you address bad food or service without a fuss?

Yes / No

10). Do you try and help others to work out their problems rather than imposing your solutions?

Yes / No

11). Do you ask for money owing from people calmly?

Yes / No

12). Do you correct people who jump the queue?

Yes / No

13). Do you find that you can count on people you know to collaborate with you?

Yes / No

14). Can you separate emotion from facts when involved in conflict resolution?

Yes / No

Rate Yourself By Counting The Positive Responses In Each Questionnaire

A - Non- Assertive/submissive

B - Aggressive

C - Assertive

Select A 1-4 Response Based On The Following Scale To The Questions

1 = Never
2 = Seldom
3 = Often
4 = Frequently

1. Does decision making come easy for you?

2. Do you tend to think your answers are always right?

3. When you meet a stranger, are you first to introduce yourself?

4. Do you find it easy to compliment others?

5. If someone makes an unreasonable demand on you, are you comfortable saying no?

6. When you differ with someone, are you able to speak up for your viewpoint?

7. Do you continue to pursue an argument after the other person has had enough?

8. Do you confront unacceptable behaviour from others?

9. Do you speak up during group discussions and debates?

10. Do you protest when someone jumps the queue in front of you?

11. Are you critical of others' opinions, or feelings?

12. Do you insist that faulty workmanship be corrected in products you purchase?

13. Do you have confidence in your own judgement?

14. Are you able to accept compliments graciously?

15. Are you quick to anger?

16. Are you able to confront others even though the situation might be embarrassing?

17. Are you able to ask colleagues and bosses for help?

18. When others are unfair, do you call it to their attention?

19. Do you insist that others live up to their responsibilities?

20. Do you tend to dominate conversations with others?

21. Do you push or bully others to get what you want.

22. Do you make others' decisions for them?

23. Do you get angry at strangers who irritate you?

24. Do you bring poor service to the attention of management?

25. Do you feel comfortable asking for a raise if you feel that you deserve it?

26. Do you tend to be the leader in a group of friends?

27. Do you feel and act self confidently?

28. I express my opinions, even if others in the group disagree with me.

29. I am able to speak openly about my feelings.

30. If I am not satisfied with the service in a restaurant, I let the waiter know.

31. I feel free to politely voice my disagreement with someone in a position of authority.

32. I have nothing to lose by asking questions in front of other people.

33. To meet new people and make new friends, one has to get out, find them and invest some time and energy.

34. If my neighbours made too much noise, I would let them know.

35. I feel comfortable saying no.

36. When I am overcharged in a store, I bring it to the cashier's attention.

37. If a friend woke me up late at night with an unimportant call, I would say that I was already sleeping and prefer not to be called so late.

38. When a friend borrows something from me and forgets to return it, I feel comfortable reminding him/her.

39. Do you finish other people's sentences for them?

40. I take a compliment very easily.

41. I think it is important to admonish others when they are wrong.

42. I find it easy to tell someone that I like him or her or that I had a good time.

43. Confrontation is better than playing for time.

44. I resist people who take advantage of me.

45. When I talk to people in positions of authority, it does not make me feel nervous, self conscious or unsure of myself.

46. I enjoy paying someone a compliment.

47. I enjoy dealing with someone who is assertive.

48. I find opinionated people amusing.

49. When I join a group, I usually take over the conversation.

50. When an argument is over, I am usually happy I said all the things I should have said at the time.

51. When I make phone calls to institutions, government agencies or businesses, I am prepared and seldom feel I did not take the opportunity to say what I should have said.

52. When I go out with someone, we do what I suggest, even though they feel like doing something else.

53. I take defective goods back to the store for a refund/exchange very easily.

54. I am able to express my discontent with a friend or partner if I think it's justified.

55. Instead of accepting responsibility for other people's mistakes, I tend to argue.

56. When a telesales person tries to sell me something, I tell them in no uncertain terms that I am not interested.

57. When I am left alone with someone who is very attractive, my conversation is much the same as with someone who I do not find attractive.

58. I find myself going over battles and conflict in my mind, honing my skills as an arguer and a victor in disputes.

59. When I have a disagreement with someone, I find myself wanting to bring the dispute to the fore, so as to settle the score.

60. If someone disappoints me or lets me down, I will not resume normal relations until we resolve the dispute.

Characteristics Of A Passive Communicator

Respects others, not self.

Others are okay, but not self.

Self put-down – can't accept compliments.

Indirect.

Hints.

Hidden bargains.

Can't confront and avoids confrontation.

Whines.

Passive aggressive.

Feels controlled.

Depressed, self pity, low self esteem, high anxiety, high defences.

Confused relationships.

Won't ask, won't say no.

Allow others to choose for him/her.

Avoids or gives in.

Characteristics Of An Assertive Communicator

Respects self, respects others.

You're OK. I'm OK.

Avoids put downs, accepts compliments.

Appropriately direct.

Requests.

Openly expresses expectations.

Confronts and accepts confrontation.

Registers complaints.

Deals openly with others.

Feels in control of self.

Contentment, positive self-concept, alive, low anxiety, low defences.

Clear relationships, strong relationships.

Asks. Does not take no personally.

Chooses for self.

Evaluates and acts.

Characteristics Of An Aggressive Communicator

Respects self, not others.

I'm OK, you're not OK.

Puts others down, uses sarcasm, pays backhanded compliments.

Inappropriately direct.

Demands.

Pressures.

Confronts but does not accept confrontations.

Accuses, attacks.

Aggresses, attacks, puts down.

Needs to control others.

Agitation, exaggerated self esteem, anxiety, defence.

Clear relationships but few. Lonely.

Asks, demands, can't take no.

Chooses for others.

Attacks.

Relationship Between Self And Others

The passive person is preoccupied with being liked and accepted. However, because the passive person usually does not accept him/herself, they are afraid to speak up for fear of rejection.

The passive person gives the power over self-acceptance to others. He/she feels powerless.

The aggressive person focuses on his her own desires and how others may be used to achieve them.

While the aggressive person usually appears to value him or herself highly, little regard is given to others, their feelings or rights.

The assertive person values him or herself but also values others. The assertive person does not necessarily like everyone nor desire to be liked by everyone, but he or she does respects others and their rights.

Those who behave in an assertive manner are comfortable with themselves and others and are then more likely to be comfortable with them.

Non-verbal Communication

Being part of the same social system does not mean we are all the same. People are unique, even people who grow up in the same family differ from each other. This makes communication a difficult and complex subject to study. We have all been programmed or conditioned to some extend by our early upbringing, our experiences and society. We know what we consider to be right, correct or good behaviour in certain circumstances.

How regularly do you take cultural differences into consideration when you communicate with others? South Africa is a multicultural society where ignorance slows our ability to develop meaningful relationships with people from other cultures. We also need to become more comfortable with the idea of talking about our differences; we must learn to share our feelings and ideas with people from diverse cultures.

Gender also has an influence on the way we communicate. As we grow up, we learn to behave within our gender roles. Men and women are pressurised to accept certain interaction patterns, and they usually develop a preference for the different communication styles. For example, women are thought to be more sensitive, emotional, caring and friendly than men, while men are frequently seen as strong, independent, assertive and unemotional.

We learn the effects of certain actions we take.

We learn all about the impression we make when we smile at people. Many of us have learned to smile at people we do not like so that we give one impression and hide another.

We learn how we can affect people by wearing different clothes and how vital this can be to first impressions in both business and social life.

We learn how to use the tone of our voice subtly to modify the meaning of our words. We can sound aggressive and menacing, or gentle and soothing. We can even change the meaning of words completely.

Non-verbal communication refers to the messages that people convey through their bodies, touch, vocal variations and their use of space, time and objects. Non-verbal communication is most important in expressing our emotions and social meaning.

When discussing communication skills we must include body language – your voice, gestures, and visual presence – and the impact it has on the communication process.

The Body Language – Mood Link

How do you sit when you are miserable? When you are excited? When you are absolutely fascinated by what someone is telling you?

Knowing how to use body language is important regardless of whether you are speaking or listening.

Consider what you say, as well as:

The tone of voice – should be confident, direct, clear.

Context – stick to what is relevant.

Body posture – relax, maintain positive eye contact.

If you study non-verbal tactics at work or socially, you will be surprised how many people use them as an aid to achieving their objectives - often seemingly subconsciously.

We do this all our lives but most of us are unaware of our skills and therefore do not try and develop them. We seem to pick up a range of skills, such as nodding, to encourage others to speak, that we are not conscious of. What we can do is become more aware of our own and other's reactions to our non-verbal communication, so that we can modify our behaviour to get the response we desire.

The listener interprets the message using the three elements of interpersonal communication:

Words/verbal: what is said

Tone: how it is said

Body language: facial expression, movement, gesture.

A message is really powerful if all these elements support each other, but what happens if these elements are in conflict? We doubt the message and the sincerity of the speaker.

If someone says:

"I love you" however warmly, without any supportive expression and movement, the message loses most of its impact and meaning. We even react to people who don't smile with their eyes.

In conclusion:

actions speak louder than words.

Tests with posture and relaxation show that they are good indicators of attitude and status towards another person. We usually incline towards people we like not only with our feelings but also with our bodies. However it is important not to make assumptions when trying to read this form of non-verbal communication but to pick up pointers and judge them in context.

It is also useful to know the normal physical behaviour of the other person. If we think of somebody we know well, we can probably think of the tell tale indicators they may make for different feelings like anger, tiredness, happiness etc.

Assertive communicators have learnt the art of using their body language and tone of voice to support the verbal message they wish to convey.

Gesture Clusters

One of the most serious mistakes a novice in body language can make is to interpret a solitary gesture in isolation of other gestures or other circumstances. For example scratching the head can mean a number of things: dandruff, fleas, sweating, uncertainty, forgetfulness or lying. Depending on the other gestures that occur at the same time, we must always look at gesture clusters for a correct reading.

Like any other language, body language consists of words, sentences and punctuation. Each gesture is a single word and a word may have several different meanings. It is only when you put the word into a sentence with other words that you can fully understand its meaning. Gestures come in "sentences" and invariably tell the truth about a person's feelings or attitudes. The "perceptive" person is one who can read the non-verbal sentences and accurately match them against the person's non-verbal sentences.

In addition to looking for gesture clusters and similarity of speech and body movement, all gestures should be considered in the context in which they occur. Voice, facial and body gestures, postures and distance – all are forms of body language. They can strengthen the way you communicate or damage it. Just as you develop and master verbal communication and listening skills, you need to master body language.

Response Skills

Although response skills are crucial to assertive communication, the cycle of effective listening is not complete without an effective response.

Two of the most important objectives of response skills are to clarify and to comfort. Repeat your understanding of the message back to the speaker to check understanding. Your response will tell them whether the intended message has been communicated. Once understanding has been established, you may need to respond further by providing emotional comfort to the speaker.

Comforting responses show approval of a person's feelings, or acknowledge the person's rights to have those feelings.

Use Factual Description Instead Of Judgement

Aggressive:

This is sloppy work

Assertive:

The pages in this report are not in the correct order.

Aggressive:

You are never on time

Assertive:

You were 15 minutes late today. That's the third time this week.

Saying No

Some of us do not have a problem with saying no, or, if we do say yes, have no problem being appreciated for it. It is other people who say yes when they would love to say no, who are easily manipulated, but who get very little thanks for their effort.

Assertiveness training does not advocate saying no beyond the point of unreasonableness; this would be aggressive and un-cooperative. Saying no most of the time does not build relationships.

What We Need Is

The skills to be able to say no when we are within our rights and it is our choice.

The ability to do so in such a way as not to destroy the relationship.

For most people who are non-assertive by nature this can be very difficult and it means that they can often be made to agree to things that they would rather refuse.

The technique of refusing people when we are within our rights can combine some of the following skills:

Broken record.

Non-verbal communication.

Active listening.

Self disclosure.

Free information.

Fogging.

Negative assertion.

The broken record is the key to saying no. With a cool, relaxed voice and other suitable non-verbal communication you calmly repeat your refusal. You focus on the intention and refuse to be sidetracked.

This can still be hard to do with a very manipulative person who plays on your values, emotions and feelings. Sometimes we can be made to feel that our refusal will damage our relationship. This is where we can combine the broken record techniques with others whilst we persist.

Self Disclosure:

I am sure I would feel very much as you do, but I cannot agree because I have made previous arrangements.

Free Information:

Well I can see that this is going to put you out, but, all the same, I have a prior arrangement.

Fogging:

You may well be right that I am being selfish this time, but I must stick to my arrangements.

Yes, I probably seem very stubborn and disloyal but I think it is important in this case because of my previous arrangements.

Negative Assertion:

Well you are right to say that I haven't done anything to help you so far, but I must really keep faith with my other arrangements this time.

Yes, I agree that I am being difficult and unhelpful but I think my previous arrangements justify my attitude.

If emotion is used against us, then the best thing to do is to use active listening. This calms the emotional side by trying to understand people's feelings (empathy) and release the analytical side of their thinking.

Mirroring

Mirroring is a way of developing rapport. When you copy the overall gestures or word patterns of the person to whom you are communicating, that person starts to get the feeling that there is something about you that they like. In your behaviour, they see a reflection of their own behaviour and this tends to set up a very solid basis for establishing and developing rapport and empathy.

Once we have matched the other person's behaviour it is then possible to lead them to reach your desired outcomes. If an employer wishes to develop an immediate rapport and create a relaxed atmosphere with an employee, he need only copy the employee's posture to achieve this end.

Similarly, an up-and-coming employee may be seen copying his boss's gestures in an attempt to show agreement.

Using this knowledge, it is possible to influence a face-to-face encounter by copying the positive gestures and postures of the other person. This has the effect of putting the other person in a receptive and relaxed frame of mind, as he can "see" that you understand his point of view.

We Can:

Match breathing – as you notice the rise and fall of the chest, get in rhythm with the other person.

Matching voice in pace and power.

Matching words.

Matching gestures.

Matching eye movement.

Helping Others Develop Assertiveness

By being assertive and having a positive attitude with others, you can help influence their behaviour.

By being assertive with people you are more likely to engage an assertive response in return. Think about the times you felt good when you handled a particular situation. How were you feeling at the time?

The likelihood is that you felt confident and behaved assertively. Think about the response from others. Usually people respond in a likeminded way, but what about those with whom you work or live who behave submissively or aggressively; can you influence them?

Communication Style

Speaking well can have a dramatic effect on your professional and private life. Whilst we have already discovered that oral communication makes up 7% of our total communication skills, we really need to make the most of our oral communication opportunities when they are presented to us. We can use rhetorical devices to liven up our communication and make them more convincing and interesting to our audience.

The word rhetorical means: using the language well. Rhetorical devices are useful. It is how something is said, not what is said that usually wins the day. Having a good idea or something to say is not enough. We must also get the message across to the intended recipients, and do it in such a way that both the message and its importance is received and understood.

Communication is always understood in the context and experience of the receiver – no matter what was intended.

Pace, Pause And Rhythm

If you speak rapidly you need to concentrate on correct breathing and pause appropriately.

Speaking rapidly is not necessarily a bad thing, but the rapid speaker has to meet several conditions to be understood. First your articulation must be clear; secondly you must breathe well, and thirdly you must use pauses effectively. Pausing allows the speaker time to recharge and it gives the listener a chance to absorb what has been said.

If you speak quickly, ask yourself why you do so. You might be nervous, or uncomfortable with silence, and therefore chatter to maintain a conscious flow of sound. You may also be enthusiastic about a subject or overflowing with ideas. Whatever the reason, you have to force yourself to pause. If you do not do so, you may become confused and may also irritate or confuse those listening to you.

A slow speaker can be just as irritating – and will bore their audience. If you notice your listener's attention wandering, you may need to speed up your pace to energise the audience.

The rhythm of your speech is also closely linked to how you breathe. It is your breathing that dictates how much energy is available for the flow of speech, and where the breaks come. Non-rhythmical speech does not sound pleasing. If your speaking rhythm is halting and jerky, broken by frequent gasps for breath; try to relax.

Pitch And Intonation

Do not confuse pitch and tone. The pitch of your voice is determined by the length and thickness of your vocal cords. You alter the length and thickness by stretching or relaxing the vocal cords. If these are restricted because of tension in the body or poor posture, your voice will sound less "full" and "rich" than it otherwise might.

Poor use of pitch can spoil a good speaking voice. Some speakers tend to stretch their voice beyond it's natural limits – resulting in a forced and unattractive sound. Others do not stretch their voices enough – and so tend to sound monotonous when they are speaking. Every voice has a natural middle tone. Learn to identify and adapt your middle tone. You will sound natural if you speak around this pitch and your intonation will also be correct.

Emphasis, Stress, Repetition, And Exclamation

As you experiment with your pitch and tone, consider your use of emphasis when you speak.

Changes in emphasis often accompany changes in pitch. The placing of emphasis often affects the meaning of a sentence.

Some people use far too much emphasis. They have a message to get across, and they try to drive it home by emphasising it repeatedly. Ironically, this often just alienates listeners rather than convincing them.

When communicating you must try and gain as much information about the person/s you are communicating with.

Evaluate A Conversation

In order to evaluate a conversation you will need to apply all the communication skills you have learned.

All conversations have to be taken in context. When evaluating oral communication you must be aware of the context in which the conversation takes place to get a true worth of the conversation.

If you are approached by someone who has a need to share information with you, determine the value of the information and the attitude of the person, then do your own investigation. Do not comment on assumptions that either yourself or the other person has made, and do not allow yourself to make assumptions about a situation based on your own values and attitudes without thinking how it might appear to others.

Communication in general has to do with getting your message across to others. Oral communication has to do with using words; words that are right for the other person. There are certain advantages and disadvantages to oral communication. One of the disadvantages, especially in a call centre, is the fact that you cannot see the other person, and therefore cannot pick up on any non-verbal messages communicated by body language and gestures.

There are different styles of communication and we should at all times try to use assertive communication if we want lasting result rather than non-assertive or aggressive communication.

It is important to remember that we choose the way in which we communicate by selecting words and tone of voice.

Guidelines For Effective Interactions

Provide sufficient information.

Provide valuable information.

Provide relevant information.

Communicate With Clarity

Organise your thoughts and use specific language that clarifies your meaning. If your listener is unable to follow what you are saying, you are not contributing to the sharing of meaning.

For example:

When someone asks you for directions to a specific place, do not give details in whatever order comes to mind. Start from a specific point, and work towards the destination in a clear and organised fashion.

Communicating with clarity also means presenting consistent verbal and non-verbal messages that reinforce one another. If you say one thing and your non-verbal signals say another, you are confusing your listener and making shared meaning less probable.

Communicate In An Ethical Way

Communicate in ways that are morally and ethically acceptable. These may differ from culture to culture, but generally acknowledged violations would include sharing information that someone has disclosed to you confidentially, or pretending to give information when you know you are not.

However, being truthful means not only avoiding deliberate lies or distortions, but also avoiding any kind of misrepresentation.

The truth is more important than the facts. Although we normally presume the two to be synonymous, there are ways to present the facts that are not strictly truthful and they lead to misconceptions in the receiver's mind.

Often cultures differ in their views of what ethical communication is. In low-context cultures, people are expected to speak their minds and tell the truth. They communicate their actual feelings about things.

People in high-context cultures try to communicate in ways that maintain harmony. Thus instead of voicing their true feelings, they may send a message that is more acceptable.

For example:

A lecturer will ask her student whether they have understood what she has been saying. Students from some black South African cultures will rather agree to have understood what she said, even when they have not, because to say that they have not understood would imply that the lecturer is at fault for not explaining the material effectively, and they would rather lie than imply this.

Communicate In A Polite Way

Be courteous to other communication participants. Politeness is common to all cultures, although levels of politeness and ways of being polite vary. It meets people's universal need to feel appreciated and protected.

Managing Conflict

Conflict is a condition of clashing interests, and can thus be seen as a purposeful interactive process in which more than one party with apparent irreconcilable aims opposes each other.

Key To Communication Styles

Aggressive/Confrontational:

Forceful
Domineering
In control
Judgmental
Argumentative
Aggressive
Tough
Explosive
Uncompromising

Assertive/Persuasive:

Proactive
Assertive
Persuasive
Communicative
Firm but fair
Problem-centred
Direct
Collaborative
Reasonable

Observant/Introspective:

Unbiased
Reflective
Analytical
Active listening
Reserved
Co-operative
Conciliatory
Balanced
Introspective

Avoiding/Reactive:

Passive
Accommodating
Easy-going
Withdrawn
Smoothing over
Apologetic
Submissive
Avoiding
Patient

Resolving Conflict

Resolving conflict in which you yourself are involved in is a major challenge since you need to control your own emotions. To do this you first need to understand your own behaviour. What follows are some questions you may ask yourself when identifying your approach to conflict.

How do you experience anger:

When you are in a conflict situation, how do you express anger when it arises?

Do you show your emotions or do you shut off and refuse to communicate?

Do you express your anger or deny it?

I'm OK – You're not OK:

This position comes across as arrogant and aggressive. It is common in conflict and is generally accompanied by an effort to collect reasons to justify why one is right and why the other party is stupid, to blame etc. It wants victory rather than resolution and is often accompanied by stereotyping and a one-sided distortion of what is happening. Anger is mistaken as strength. Power tactics are seen as the best way of protecting one's interests. This position can easily become biased or racist.

I'm not OK – You're OK:

This position comes across as weak and submissive and can attempt to manipulate the situation through self-pity. It leads to helplessness, but those who hold this position

can be strong in their weakness and resist attempts to change them. Interlocking positions can emerge when this position gets into conflict with the first one. People in this position often feel like victims and aren't prepared to take responsibility.

I'm Not OK – You're not OK:

This position can combine low self-esteem with a negative view of the other party. It has no faith in conflict resolution and would incline to lose-lose attitudes. It is often the result of chronic unresolved conflicts that have hit deadlock and resulted in despair or depression.

Both parties may have used questionable methods and have given up trying to make a difference. It is often accompanied by disruptive passive resistance which undermined communication, productivity etc.

I'm OK – You're OK:

This is the only balanced and positive life position. This attitude does not depend on the behaviour of the other party but comes from inner strength. It allows one to maintain one's balance through stepping back from the emotional turmoil of the conflict and staying positive. This is the basis of real strength and is difficult to sustain under frustrating conditions. Without this position it is almost impossible to resolve conflicts either between oneself and others, or between others. To achieve balance it is generally necessary to separate the people from the problem.

Do You Have To Be In Control

Being in control of the situation is not always as advantageous as we believe it to be if we attempt to take responsibility for other people's behaviour. Being in control of ourselves on the other hand is extremely useful.

To use an example:

If the road is covered with thorns we can either cover the whole road with leather or else we can use much less leather and cover our feet.

Steps To Follow In Resolving Your Own Conflict

Recognise your own emotions.

Separate the personal emotional stuff from the actual problem: be soft on the people and hard on the problem.

Look for the real need/interests in the situation. Avoid an US and THEM situation.

Look for win-win solutions and options for mutual benefit.

Apply fair standards and don't resort to a battle of wills.

Adopt a problem solving approach.

Decide on practical solutions – set objectives.

Make peace, forgive, move on.

Resolving Conflict Between Others

This involves listening to people so that they feel heard and so that any built-up emotions are released. People are rarely ready to move on to solutions until their emotional blocks have been removed.

Not every difference of opinion is characterised by intense emotions. There are people who objectively face issues, calmly discuss the facts, listen politely to each other and collaborate to find the best solution.

Common Behaviour Patterns In Conflict Situations

People pushing their points of view without being at all receptive to the ideas of others.

People becoming angry, defensive and personal with each other.

Negative body language like glaring and pointing fingers.

Sarcastic or dismissive remarks.

People butting heads and criticizing each other's ideas.

Quiet people withdrawing emotionally to avoid becoming involved.

Extreme anger to the point where relationships are damaged.

It is the facilitator's job to handle negative emotions effectively as soon as they emerge so that they don't effect or mar the dynamics of the group. When emotions set in at the beginning, the facilitator should employ some of the following basic strategies:

Slow things down:

Get the attention of people by stopping the action and asking them to slow down. You can use the excuse that you can't take notes as quickly as people are talking. Ask them to start over and repeat key ideas.

Stay totally neutral:

Never take sides or allow you body language to hint that you favour one idea or one person over another.

Stay Calm:

Maintain your composure and do not raise your voice. Speak slowly with an even tone.

Avoid emotional body language.

Revise the Norms:

Point out the existing norms and remind people that they had agreed to them earlier on.

Be Assertive:

Move into the referee mode. Insist that people speak one at a time. Stop people who interrupt others. Don't stand by passively whilst others engage in an argument and debate.

Raise Awareness:

Record ideas that unfold about the difference between a debate and an argument.

Ask them whether they would prefer to engage in an argument or a debate.

Make Interventions:

Don't allow people to argue with each other or display rudeness.

Emphasize Listening:

Paraphrase key points and ask others to do the same.

Call Time Out:

Don't hesitate to stop the action any time emotions get out of hand or if the discussion is spinning in circles.

Use the Flip Chart:

Make note of key points so that they are at hand and the group members don't have to go into discussion again. Whenever you need to regain control for a few minutes, read the notes on the flip chart.

Create Closure:

Make sure that the debating is really going somewhere. Ask people to help summarize what has been agreed to. Test these items for agreement. Help the group create action plans to ensure implementation of key suggestions.

Listen – Empathise – Clarify – Seek Permission – Resolve

Listen:

Instead of arguing when you hear a point you disagree with, listen attentively to the person's main points. Allow people to vent their feelings. Look interested and concerned. Say any of these things "tell me more. That's interesting. Uh-huh. I'm not sure I understand. Could you go over that again?"

Empathise:

Accept the views of the other person even if you don't agree with them. Let people know you understand their feelings. Say "I don't blame you for feeling that way. I see what you mean. I understand how you feel. I'm sure I would feel the same way if..."

Clarify:

Delve deeper to ensure that you have a clear understanding of what the other person is saying to you. Say "Let me see if I've got it straight; what you're saying is... Is it possible that... The idea you're proposing is..."

Seek Permission:

Tell your side after the other person has expressed all of his/her concerns and feels clearly understood. Say "Now that I understand your views, can I explain mine?" "It seems that this would be a good time to bring up a few points you haven't mentioned".

Resolve the Issue:

Once you have both heard each other, it is time to start dealing with the problem together.

Resolving Issues

Choose the appropriate structured approach to get solutions. This can be a collaborative problem-solving activity, compromising, accommodating or consciously avoiding.

Once emotions have been vented, and in order to resolve the underlying issue, the following five basic approaches can be used:

Avoid:

Ignore the conflict in the hope that it will go away. Maintain silence or try to change the subject.

Accommodate:

Ask people to be more tolerant and accept each other's views. Ask them to try and get along with each other. This sometimes involves asking one person to give in to another person.

Compromise:

Look for the middle ground between highly polarised views. Ask each person to give up some of what he/she wants, in order to get other items he/she thinks are more important.

Compete:

Use force to make points and quell any conflicts. Go for personal win even if the other person feels like he/she has lost the argument.

Collaborate:

Face the conflict and draw people's attention to it. Surface the issues and resolve them in a win-win way by using systematic problem solving.

Customer Service Course

The main focus of this course is to provide the necessary skills for effective customer service.

The most important people in any successful organization are the staff. Without properly trained and motivated staff no company can provide an effective service to their customers.

Well trained staff have confidence and enjoy their work. They are more effective in what they do, and are more capable to meet customer requirements.

Training should be an ongoing process, and not just a once off event. It should become part of the company culture, and the accepted way of doing business.

The Main Purpose of Staff Training:

Effective Communication.

Listening Skills.

Customer Loyalty.

What Type Of Training Should Be Provided?

Each company has unique requirements that vary greatly.

What do you want to achieve with the training?

What type of business do you have?

You need to have a clear idea of exactly what you are looking for.

Companies need to establish how their customers gather and exchange information. They no longer can afford the dictum of "we have always done it like this".

There is a vast variety of ways to communicate with customers ranging from traditional methods to modern online methods.

A company's commitment to Customer Service dictates that it caters for its customers' needs. The definition of customer service: the ability of an organisation to consistently and constantly exceed the customer's expectations. A small business can distinguish itself from the competition by providing excellent customer service. It requires a commitment to learn what the customer's needs and wants are and developing action plans that implement customer friendly processes.

In order to accept this definition we have to recognise that every aspect of the business has an impact on customer service that also involves face-to-face customer contact.

Business owners have to place a lot of faith and trust in their staff to provide the type of service that will leave the customer feeling happy and satisfied. Staff also have to recognise that they will not be able to satisfy every customer no matter how helpful and accommodating they are.

Good customer service should be the priority of any company. They have to put in place proper guidelines for staff and provide the necessary training.

Important Points To Consider

What is the main goal:

Do you mainly conduct business over the phone, or do the staff interact with customers directly?

Define your expectations:

Employees need to know exactly what is expected from them.

Define objectives clearly.

Provide the tools necessary to achieve these objectives.

Be specific – don't assume that employees know what you expect from them.

Provide the necessary tools:

Employees cannot be effective if they do not have the necessary tools at their disposal. This can include access to email, a mobile phone, up to date computer equipment and software.

Ensure they know how to use these tools.

Set Boundaries:

Your employees need to know and understand company policies and procedures.

Practical Training:

Give examples of actual incidents, and get the staff involved in providing suggestions on resolving the problem. Enlist the assistance of your most successful staff in the training.

The Importance Of Role Play

Provide employees the opportunity to role play their responses. This will give them a higher level of confidence when a real situation occurs and they will be able to respond more effectively.

Handling Difficult Clients

Learning to deal with difficult customers can provide you with valuable information, and assist with improving your customer service standards. There are often valid points and issues behind the complaints. They can be your best source for information on service improvement. Pleasing your difficult clients will result in consistent and satisfying customer service for an average client.

Failures And Successes

You should focus on both. Celebrate the successes and analyze the failures. Treat each failure as an opportunity to learn, and how it can be avoided in future. What lessons can be learned from these failures? This will create a good balance and serve to build a strong customer service culture.

Share success stories. Discussions around these issues can often provide the best training, and can be used for role playing.

Lead by Example:

The manner in which you deal with customers will send a strong message to your staff.

Ensure that the example you set is worth following.

Effective Communication

Effective communication is crucial for any company. You have to keep up with the times whilst taking care not to neglect customers who prefer more traditional ways of communication.

Communication can be defined as follows:

Expression plus comprehension = communication.

Communication should be a two way street. Communicate with your customers and allow them to communicate with you. Their feedback is important and has a fundamental impact on how we manage our business, develop policies or products.

If it is the type of business where you deal with customers one-on-one, you have the added advantage of observing their body language which will provide valuable clues, and enable you to deal with them effectively.

They touch you on the arm – are they being affectionate or insecure?

Hands on hips – they are being patronizing or judgemental – did you offend them?

Arms crossed – they are closed off – you have lost them.

Arched eyebrows – surprised or confused – you need to take control.

Pointing a finger – accusatory – you need to fix the problem fast.

By paying close attention to posture and facial expression you can quickly assess how to deal with the situation.

If you do not meet your clients directly you can communicate with them through questionnaires and surveys. You can use Newsletters, Websites or emailed messages.

Customers will remain loyal if they feel that you value their input and opinions. Knowing what your customers feel and think can be a very powerful tool.

What are you saying and how are you saying it? Take time to focus on telling people in a way that you would want to hear it. Relay information to people in a positive way without lying, exaggeration or distortion.

Welcome your customers with a friendly greeting.

Establish the purpose of the visit.

Interact with them on their terms.

Add the personal touch. Enquire how they are.

Ask for their input.

Advise them on the services the company has to offer.

Include them in all communications regarding their service experience.

Involve them.

Interview them: Find out their exact requirements.

Invest your time to discover what will work best for your client.

Provide meaningful dialogue with your client.

Use your instincts to discover better ways to provide excellent customer service.

Do not compromise on the quality of the service.

Protect your customer's rights.

Exceed their expectations.

Be courteous: say "please" and "thank you".

Do not use negatives like "No", "You will have to" or "We don't do that".

Be enthusiastic in your approach.

Become invaluable to your client.

Treat your clients like friends.

Get feedback from your clients about the service they received.

Act on this information to get change implemented where necessary.

Always look for ways to improve service.

Be creative in your approach.

Develop an ongoing strategy with your customers.

Invent new ways to provide an effective service.

Develop and evaluate ingenious ways to work out solutions to difficult problems.

Make self evaluation an integral part of your day. What could have been done differently or how do you want it to turn out?

Integrate service solutions with good manners and appropriate language. Do not use slang

Initiate all communications with customers where possible.

Provide interim solutions that bridge gaps. Do not wait for it to become a problem.

Actions are better than intentions. Be pro-active.

Keep communication open.

Emphasise the benefits the customer can expect in working with you.

Be ethical in your approach.

Inspire your customer by Leading them, by Asking them, by Providing them with the best service you can offer.

Telephonic Customer Service

Dealing with customers over the phone can sometimes be challenging.

Here is 10 Golden Rules for Telephone Technique.

Identify the company and yourself. Show that you care about the person you are talking to.

Have a smile in your voice. Placing a mirror on your desk will heighten your awareness.

Pay attention to your tone and voice. It will help create an impression of enthusiasm, and help the caller to get a clear understanding of what you are saying.

Have a warm greeting and opening.

Have a strong closing. Never put the phone down without saying goodbye.

Avoid technical jargon. Keep it simple and to the point.

Stay Calm. Never respond on an emotional level when dealing with an irate customer. You lose your cool – you lose control.

If you have to transfer the call first ensure the person you are transferring to is available.

Avoid putting callers on hold.

If you have to put the caller on hold inform them on how long the wait will be. It is better to call them back within a specified time. Always keep that promise.

Dealing With Difficult Customers

Dealing with irate customers can be intimidating and frustrating.

Always deal with problems immediately.

Investigate the course of the problem and how to prevent it from happening again.

Treat your customers with dignity. That does not mean that you have to let them walk all over you. Address real problems and fix them well. Point out unrealistic expectations in a calm and reasonable manner.

Exceed their expectations. By delivering more than expected you will get more repeat business and word of mouth advertising.

Never make excuses. Admit mistakes and never try and shift blame. This approach will impress your customer.

Don't take it personally. The customer's anger is not directed at your personally – you just happen to be in the line of fire! Stay calm and take control.

Listen to your customers. Never make assumptions. Let them speak. Do not interrupt. Never over promise. It is better to surprise than to disappoint.

Make certain you can deliver on your promises.

Make the customer feel that they are a priority. Pay close attention to what they say.

Never ignore a problem in the hope that it will go away. It never does – you have to solve it.

Always follow up. If it was a problem: Are they happy with the way in which it was resolved? If they placed a large order: were they happy with the service they have received?

These simple steps will make you stand out from the crowd, and go a long way in building lasting relationships with your customers.

Listening Skills

We often hear what the customer is saying, but are we actually listening to what they are saying?

How often has this happened to you?

You place a meal order in a restaurant. You order a medium rump steak with salad. The waiter repeats the order back to you. When your food arrives the steak is underdone! You are left feeling irritated and frustrated. Why didn't they listen to me?

You and seven of your friends go out to dinner. Your meal and drinks orders are taken.

Nothing is written down yet every order arrives exactly as ordered! How is that possible?

Your waiter listened to you.

Listening is one of the most important tools to get to know your customers, understand their needs, and get to the core of their problems. It allows us to provide a better service and produce results.

Acknowledge the benefits of listening carefully to your customer.

Do not allow any distractions when the customer is talking.

Stay 100% focussed.

Establish frequent eye contact.

Remain focussed when dealing with customers over the phone.

Write key words down so that you will retain the main ideas.

Never interrupt.

Keep your emotions in check.

Pay attention to the customer's body language.

If you do not understand completely ask the customer to repeat.

Rephrase and double check with the customer.

By applying these points you will communicate more effectively and have a better understanding of their expectations.

NEVER say:

Our system is down…

I tried but…

We are having a staffing problem…

We have been very busy…

We can't do that…

Our policy is…

The rules are…

Rather use:

Thank you for your feedback.

We learn from our customers input.

We can certainly learn from your suggestions and improve.

I will ensure the right people get your feedback.

What can I do to win back your trust?

Create a profile for each customer. This will establish common ground and provide a personal touch. Make the experience a pleasant one.

People do business with people they know and trust. Establish trust with your clients.

Listen carefully so that you have a clear understanding of their needs.

Adjust your communication style to theirs.

Deliver on your promises. Fulfil that commitment on time.

Always under promise and over deliver.

Do not waste time with small talk when you are dealing with people who are goal orientated.

How do you deal with your customers?

Do you find exceptional ways to exceed your customers' expectations?

Do you always find a way to connect and make their day?

Do you turn complaints into compliments and always approach problems in a positive way?

If you are doing all of these – you are a winner.

Complaints:

Do customers complain about you or your company, or do you always complain about your colleagues?

If you are receiving lots of written testimonials and thank you letters you are handling these in the appropriate manner.

Recurring problems should be pre-empted by putting effective systems in place.

Repeat sales are a good indicator that your service is efficient and effective.

Complaints provide an opportunity to rescue the situation, learn from them and improve your service. Ignoring a problem does not make it go away – it will eventually spin out of control.

Create momentum and desire to fix the problem when you receive a complaint.

Call the customer, thank them for the complaint, and explain to them how the issue is being resolved. Complaints are the wake-up call for every company that there may be a service issue.

Keep a record of complaints and the way in which they were resolved. This is a valuable tool when a problem recurs with new staff.

If you have a recurring problem because of factors outside your control, and you know that the customer will be dissatisfied, you can turn these situations into a positive by following these guidelines:

Have brainstorming sessions around these ideas.

Record all ideas.

Keep it positive – don't just look at the problem also find the solution.

Allow everyone to participate.

Decide which ideas you are going to try first.

Act upon these decisions.

Do regular reviews and fine tune the process.

Technology:

Modern technology can be used to great advantage. Do a bit of "snooping" to find out how the majority of your customers like to communicate.

Most companies have a website. Find yours and respond to complaints and compliments – be honest.

Make it easy for your customers to contact you via new media – where possible, make it interactive.

Use new technology to research what other companies are doing.

Write your own blog and allow feedback.

Create an environment where people feel comfortable giving you feedback.

Ask power questions that will prompt people to tell you how they really feel e.g. "What can we do better?" and " if there was one thing we could do what would it be?"

Ask them to be honest in their feedback because that is the only way you are able to improve.

Technology enables us to record personal detail about the customer that enables us to provide them with a personalised service like greeting them by name and enquiring about the family by name.

Not everyone is willing to tell you that they are unhappy, but rest assured that they will be telling all their friends and family about the bad experience they have had.

Make a list of everything you think your customers want. Next time show it to them and ask them if they would like to add anything to the list, or whether they think you have got it right. Where practical implement these suggestions.

How To Get Referrals

Always do what you say you are going to do.

Be punctual.

Always say please and thank you.

If you make a promise it is up to you to keep that promise. People are often reluctant to take responsibility. It is so much easier to blame a supplier, technology, colleagues, and internal politics. How about taking ownership of the situation and making it happen.

Respect other people's time by being on time. Plan your day. If you have to drive to meet someone - allow for traffic congestion by leaving earlier than required. How often have you heard someone say "there is not enough hours in a day"?

Ask friends and colleagues to point out when you don't say please and thank you. Say it sincerely.

Is The Customer Always Right?

Of course not. Customers will often try to exploit a situation, especially if the person helping them is uncertain and lacks confidence. For example: a customer is returning an item for credit but has exceeded the return policy's time limit. Explain to them why the goods cannot be returned for credit in a clear and empathic way with conviction in your voice. They do not want to hear "it is company policy". You have to believe in what you tell them and tell them in a firm but polite manner. People prefer dealing with confident people and like to be guided and led by them. Never be arrogant.

In order to be confident you have to know your stuff. Become an expert in the way you work, your products, your methods and your systems. Every time you use a tool or an action it becomes easier, and with that comes confidence.

First Impressions

You have only one chance to make a first impression. Make it a lasting one.

Dress appropriately. Nothing over the top. Smart conservative is normally the best route to go.

Well groomed hair – no wild colours or styles.

Bad posture creates a very bad first impression – no slouching or resting on elbows.

If you wear spectacles ensure they are well aligned and clean.

Personal hygiene is crucial – body odour and bad breath can clear a room fast.

Have a firm handshake.

Staff Empowerment

Set a budget – this way staff will know how much they can invest in time and money to solve a problem.

Share what others have done to solve a problem.

Examine past problems and the solutions applied to solve these.

Create a "no fail" environment – if someone has taken the initiative and failed – rather use it as a learning curve than view it as a failure.

Encourage staff to be pro active rather than reactive.

The Competition

Have a close look at your competition. What is their approach? Do some mystery shopping and gain first-hand experience of their operation. Then go back and see what can be done to improve. Get a professional company to do mystery shopping at your company. Advise your staff that you will be doing that – by being aware they will be focussed on their actions and you will already have
improved your service. Look at the results you receive, discuss and analyse in a positive manner.

Become multi-skilled.

Brilliance should be your benchmark.

Be prepared.

Aspire to greatness.

Take a risk – try new things.

Do not tolerate excuses.

The competition is the company where the staff

Answers the phone quicker

Delivers an order quicker.

Exceeds expectation on a more regular basis.

Sounds better and friendlier over the phone.

Lives values more passionately.

Has a clearer understanding of the customer's needs.

Goes an extra five miles when the customer is expecting one.

Customers today expect more from less. They will compare your services with recent experiences.

Most of your competitors will provide poor customer service.

How can you stand out from the crowd? By delivering outstanding service.

Dealing With Awkward Customers

Very few people will purposely be difficult. Often there are other factors that influence their behaviour and exacerbate their frustration and irritation.

Step 1:

Listen carefully, nod frequently, repeat key phrases of information, tilt your head slightly to one side, and make notes. All of these actions indicate to the client that you are actively listening.

Step 2:

Empathise. Use phrases like " I am really sorry about that" and then suggest a way to help. Asking the customer what they would like you to do about it can be construed as antagonistic and should be avoided. As the expert you should know what you can do about it. Offer a couple of suggestions before giving the customer the opportunity to tell you what their expectations are. For example "would you like a replacement product?" followed by "is there something else I can do for you right now?" Let them vent. You don't have to take the blame for someone else's problems. Remain calm and in control. Stay creative and solution orientated to ensure you do the right thing during these stressful situations.

Say sorry and mean it.

Offer a positive solution.

Follow up to make sure your customer is happy.

Your service must be so good that you end up being friends, and not just customer and service provider.

In this instance you are the brand. It is just the company logo that goes on stationery and ads.

Never allow yourself a day where you are not being the best you can be.

You must have rock solid values.

Why are you loyal to some brands and not others? Do more of what attracts you and less of what repels you.

Know your customers.

Know your product.

Get everyone involved.

Use humour.

Service Values

Service values are critical to the success of any company. Make certain that staff know and understand the service values of the company.

Most companies have a mission statement. Values are different. Everyone should have input because when you really live these values, decision making is easier, people are clear on wider objectives and customers benefit from them.

Have a close look at a good customer service experience you have had and how you can apply it in your organisation. Go to various shops and find out how it should NOT be done and apply it.

Encourage team members to do the same.

I have been into a specific shop in Centurion on three occasions and every time the experience has been the same. Staff congregated around the pay point eating and drinking, and busy on personal calls on their mobile phones. Not once was I approached and asked if I needed assistance. Amount spend in store – zero!

Another example of how not to do it. I wanted to purchase two pairs of shoes and went into a large and well known department store. I selected the shoes I wanted and went to a pay point. The staff (busy chatting) re-directed me to another pay point. As I approached the cashier looked up, gave me a large, friendly smile, greeted me, and sent me back to the group of chatting cashiers! I smiled back, and politely informed her that I have tried them already, put the shoes on the counter, bid her good day and left (after I told her I will be going to another store to make my purchase). In this instance her friendliness was appreciated, but still no gold medal for good service and no sale. She did not make the effort to establish her client's needs.

If you do not create a culture of service excellence you and your customers can become frustrated quickly. You must be at the leading edge when it comes to creating outstanding customer service.

Remember your competition may be just around the corner.

Ask yourself and your team what is important to them, and what do they think is important to the customers.

Look for themes; identify words that can be used as values e.g. be different, wow your customers.

Look for key words e.g. Magic, accurate, brilliant, consistent.

Prioritise on key words you and the team think may work.

Write descriptions.

Make them part of your culture.

Using Scripts

Scripts make customer service easier when they are delivered passionately and sincerely. It gives continuity and gives confidence. You say the right thing, you say it effortlessly, and in most cases you know what the results will be.

However, do not follow them blindly. Adapt them so that they fit in with the customer you are dealing with. Even the best script can be improved to get the most out of a situation.

Write them down – think about the words you like to use and the way they flow.

Read it aloud. Make small adjustments. Once it is committed to memory it flows easily.

Be prepared to deviate slightly but generally stick to the basic script.

Instead of greeting a customer with the standard "Can I help you?" – of course they need help – rather ask what you can do for them.

Answering Systems

Often when you phone a company or a person you end up either with a voice message, answering service, or an automated call queue system. Nowadays you get subjected to listening to music of their choice (you happen to hate it) or the standard "sorry I am not available right now.

Please leave your name and number, and I will call you back", or even worse a long convoluted unfunny funny that prompts you to cut the call there and then.

Keep your message short and unique and relevant to what you do. Out of office replies should include a what to do and who to contact if it is urgent otherwise they may end up calling the competition.

Put some thought into how you answer the phone. Phone some companies and see how they do it.

Do you just get a bored "hello" or company name? There is some real shockers out there. What can you do to sound more animated?

Sit or stand up.

Look upwards.

Smile – they can hear it in your voice.

Stay focused.

Create a visual image of the person you are speaking to.

Use the person's name.

Listen for key words like urgently, what does it cost, can I return this. Use these in the way you

Respond:

We will send it urgently; the fees are; yes, you can return it.

End the call with a sincere thank you.

To be effective you need to understand people's primary styles;

Visual

Auditory

Kinaesthetic

When speaking over the phone visual people will use visual cues like "I have seen your brochure".

They normally tend to talk quickly.

An auditory person will use cues like "I have heard about.." Auditory people tend to be more paced and usually have a wider vocabulary.

Kinaesthetic people will say things like "I know about your product" and tend to speak slowly.

Do not jump in and try to finish the sentence for them. Allow them the time to verbalise.

People feel comfortable with people like them. By understanding the personality type you are speaking to enables you to adept to a style similar to theirs and one they will be comfortable with, thereby creating a much better customer experience.

Verbal Cues To Watch Out For

Visual	Auditory	Kinaesthetic
See	Sounds	Feel
Look	Listen	Hard
Picture	Hear	Get a handle
Vision	Deaf	Touch
Reveal	Rings a bell	Grasp
Imagine	Silence	Concrete
Show	Deafening	Stroke
Clear	Tune in	Finger
Image	Hush	Gut

Most people are a combination of these three, but will always have a primary communication style. Listen for these verbal cues and focus on them. Try it out on family and friends until you feel comfortable identifying the primary communication styles.

Allow your customers to tell their story.

Actively listen. Ask questions and make the moment real.

Share what you have learned with your colleagues.

Be in the moment.

Using a person's name on a consistent basis helps you to remember their name. It personalises the service. Do not hesitate to ask people how to spell their name or surname. It shows that you are paying attention to detail and that you care. Always make a conscious effort to get the person's name. People generally treat their friends better than they treat strangers.

Use repetition and say their names at least 3 times in the first few minutes.

Create a visual image that links their name to a prominent part of their appearance.

Service Delivery

If you can save your customers time you are providing better service. Where ever you go you invariably end up in a queue. Most people's pet hate. People want service and they want it now.

Put yourself in the customer's shoes and ask yourself how long you would be prepared to wait. Then halve it.

Look at your process. Look at ways to save time.

Create a list and a plan.

Ensure that you are not compromising quality for speed.

Test these ideas to make sure they work.

Review on a regular basis.

Call Centres

It is essential for any company to have an effective call centre service. It will require a careful look at how customers prefer to communicate and operators should provide up to date information to it's customers. The general purpose of a call centre is to answer incoming calls from customers to take orders, answer inquiries and questions, handle complaints, troubleshoot problems and provide information.

The effectiveness of the system can be undermined by enforcing unrealistic call duration limits that force customers to call back several times leaving them frustrated and irritated.

Call centre operators should be proficient in relevant computer applications, have a good knowledge of customer service principles and practices, have good keyboard skills, a knowledge of administration and clerical processes, and have the relevant product knowledge.

Skills required:

Verbal and written communication skills

Listening skills

Problem analysis

Problem solving

Customer service orientation

Organizational skills

Attention to detail

Initiative

Judgement

Adaptability

Team work

Stress tolerance

Resilience

Main responsibilities:

Answer phones professionally

Respond to customer inquiries

Research required information using available resources

Handle and resolve customer complaints

Provide customers with product and service information

Process orders, forms and applications

Route calls to appropriate resource

Identify and escalate priority issues

Follow up customer calls where necessary

Complete call logs

Complete call reports

The general purpose of an outbound call centre is to interact by phone with outside parties to

solicit orders, make appointments, collect information or conduct follow-up.

Main responsibilities:

Contact businesses or individuals by phone

Deliver prepared sales scripts

Describe products and services

Respond to questions

Obtain customer information

Obtain possible customer leads

Data capture and maintenance of customer data bases

Follow up on initial contacts

Maintain records of telephonic interactions, orders and accounts

Customer Loyalty Programs

Providing exceptional customer service is still a vital ingredient for any business. In an effort to attract more customers, customer loyalty programs have become very popular. This simple business strategy targets customers who tend to buy the same or similar products on a regular basis.

Customers like the idea of being offered a reward or free product. This encourages the customer to return for repeat business.

Businesses who make the effort and time to connect with the customer have found the key to an effective loyalty program. The goal of these processes are: find, attract and win new clients, nurture and retain existing clients and entice former clients back.

www.ingramcontent.com/pod-product-compliance
Lightning Source LLC
Chambersburg PA
CBHW051221170526
45166CB00005B/1994